Mighty Machines

TRACTORS
AND FARM VEHICLES

Jean Coppendale

FIREFLY BOOKS

A FIREFLY BOOK

Published by Firefly Books Ltd. 2010

Second printing, 2012

Publisher Cataloging-in-Publication Data (U.S.)

Coppendale, Jean.
   Tractors and farm vehicles : mighty machines / Jean Coppendale.
[24] p. : col. photos. ; cm.
Includes index.
Summary: A fun book about tractors and farm vehicles for young readers, including combine harvesters, seed drills and tractor pulls.
ISBN-13: 978-1-55407-620-8 (pbk.)
1. Tractors – Juvenile literature. 2. Farm tractors – Juvenile literature. I. Title.
[E] 629.225 dc22   TL233.15C677 2010

Library And Archives Canada Cateloguing in Publication

A CIP record for this book is available from Library and Archives Canada

Published in the United States by
Firefly Books (U.S.) Inc.
P.O. Box 1338, Ellicott Station
Buffalo, New York 14205

Published in Canada by
Firefly Books Ltd.
66 Leek Crescent
Richmond Hill, Ontario L4B 1H1

Printed in China

Author Jean Coppendale
Designer Joita Das (Q2A Media)
Editor Katie Bainbridge
Picture Researcher Jyoti Sachdev (Q2A Media)

Publisher Steve Evans
Creative Director Zeta Davies
Senior Editor Hannah Ray

Picture credits
Key: t = top, b = bottom, c = center,
l = left, r = right, FC = front cover
CLAAS KGaA ltd: 5t; Dave Reede/**AGStockUSA:** 6–7;
Mirek Weichsel/**AGStockUSA:** 10–11;
Index Stock Imagery/ Photolibrary: 10b;
Agripictures: 13t; Dave Reede/**AGStockUSA:** 14–15;
Holt Studios: 15t; **CLAAS:** 16–17;
New Holland: 18–19; **Valtra:** 20–21

Words in **bold** can be found in the glossary on page 23.

Contents

What is a **tractor?**

cab

The cab has large windows so the driver can see what is happening.

This tractor is pulling a heavy trailer across a field.

Tractors are big machines that are used mostly on farms. They help farmers prepare their land and plant, care for and **harvest** their crops.

A tractor has a **cab**. The driver sits in the cab. Other machines can be hooked onto the back of a tractor, so it can do many different jobs.

Watch those wheels!

A tractor has big wheels, so it can travel across bumpy fields. The huge wheels also help stop the tractor from sinking into mud.

Some tractors have two or even three sets of wheels on each side.

Tractor wheels are made to grip soft, muddy ground.

Preparing the fields

Farmers need to prepare their fields before they can plant **crops**. To do this, farmers attach a **plow** to the back of a tractor.

A plow is a long row of metal blades. The blades turn as they are pulled through the ground.

The plow has sharp **blades** that cut through the dirt. The tractor pulls the plow through the fields. The plow blades chop up the dirt and turn it over. The plow makes rows of ditches, or **furrows**.

Sowing the seeds

When the fields are prepared, farmers plant,
or sow, seeds. They do this with a seed drill.
A seed drill is a container, or row of containers,
that is attached to the back of a tractor.
The containers are filled with seeds.

This seed drill is being
filled with corn seeds.

As the seed drill is pulled across the fields by the tractor, seeds are dropped into the furrows in the ground.

The seed drill plants the seeds in straight rows.

Taking care of the crops

Once they start growing, the new crops need to be cared for. Some farmers spray their crops with a special liquid. The liquid stops bugs from eating the plants. The liquid also stops weeds from growing.

Some farmers do not spray their crops. Instead, workers remove weeds with their hands as they are pulled through the fields.

A machine called a crop sprayer can be hooked to the back of a tractor. As the tractor moves through the fields, liquid is sprayed on the growing crops.

A crop sprayer has long arms on each side. The liquid sprays out of these arms.

Harvest time

When crops are fully grown, they must be harvested. Different machines are used to harvest different crops. Vegetable harvesters dig up vegetables that grow under the ground.

The green tractor is pulling a machine that harvests potatoes.

Vegetable harvesters pull vegetables out of the ground. Then the vegetables are dropped into a truck.

Some harvesters can dig up two rows of carrots at a time.

Collecting wheat

Wheat is ready to harvest when it is tall and **ripe**. This is done with a machine called a combine harvester. The front of a combine harvester has sharp blades that spin around.

Many combine harvesters work together to harvest large fields.

As the blades of a combine harvester spin, they cut the long stalks of wheat.

The wheat is sucked into the harvester. The **grain** of the wheat is separated from its stalk inside the harvester.

Baling hay

After a field of wheat has been harvested, the cut stalks are left behind — this is called hay. A special machine called a baler cuts the hay and makes it into round or square **bales**.

The bales of hay are tied up tightly and dropped out of the baler.

New Holland

BR560

A tractor loads the bales of hay onto a trailer. The bales are then taken away to be stored.

The hay is used as food for farm animals. During the winter, hay is also used as bedding for the animals.

Pull, tractor!

Tractors can be used for work — and for play! Tractor pulls are very exciting. People watch tractor pulls to see which tractor will pull the heaviest weight.

The tractors race on a special **track**. They have huge back wheels to stop them from slipping. The tractors pull a heavy load behind them while the crowd cheers.

During a pull, a tractor's front wheels may lift off the ground.

21

Activities

- Would you like to be a farmer who drives a big tractor? Would it be fun? Would it be hard work? Draw a picture of yourself driving a tractor.

- Here are two tractors you have seen in this book. Can you remember what jobs they do?

- Write a story about a runaway tractor. How will your story start? Who will be in your story? What happens at the end? Can you draw a picture to go with your story?

- Look through the book again. Write a list of jobs that are done on the farm and the machines you need to do them. How many different machines are needed? Which job do you think would be your favorite? Why?

Glossary

Bales
Large bundles of cut hay that are tied up very tightly.

Blades
Sharp, flat pieces of metal used for cutting.

Cab
The place where the tractor driver sits and uses the controls to move the tractor.

Crops
Plants that farmers grow, such as vegetables or wheat.

Furrows
Long, narrow cuts in the ground made by a plow.

Grain
The part of the wheat that is used to make flour for bread. Grains are like tiny seeds.

Harvest
To cut and collect all the crops that are fully grown or ripe.

Plow
A machine that breaks up the dirt and prepares it for seeds to be planted.

Ripe
Crops that are fully grown and ready to harvest.

Track
A special path where tractors race.

Index